BEAUTIFUL CHILDREN
WITH PET FOXES

beautiful children with pet foxes

Jennifer LoveGrove

BOOKTHUG
2017

Canada Council for the Arts **Conseil des Arts du Canada** Funded by the Government of Canada Financé par le gouvernement du Canada

ONTARIO ARTS COUNCIL
CONSEIL DES ARTS DE L'ONTARIO
an Ontario government agency
un organisme du gouvernement de l'Ontario

The production of this book was made possible through the generous assistance of the Canada Council for the Arts and the Ontario Arts Council. BookThug also acknowledges the support of the Government of Canada through the Canada Book Fund and the Government of Ontario through the Ontario Book Publishing Tax Credit and the Ontario Book Fund.

Library and Archives Canada Cataloguing in Publication
LoveGrove, Jennifer, author
Beautiful children with pet foxes / Jennifer LoveGrove.
Poems.
Issued in print and electronic formats.
ISBN 978-1-77166-286-4 (softcover)
ISBN 978-1-77166-287-1 (HTML)
ISBN 978-1-77166-288-8 (PDF)
ISBN 978-1-77166-289-5 (Kindle)
I. Title.
PS8573.O8754B43 2017   C811'.6   C2016-908125-7   C2016-908126-5

cover image by Richard Anhert
author photograph by Sharon Harris

PRINTED IN CANADA

Contents

Incident Report: Describe the Dwelling 7

Dinner Table 8

Self-Portrait as a Mollusk 9

The Stains I Scrubbed from the Floor 10

Dream Specimen 23 12

I Know My Own Limits and They Are Rigid 15

Wipe Clean the Sky 16

When I Was Four I Put a Tent Pole Through 17
My Cheek

Self-Portrait on a Tuesday 19

Hypochondria 20

Suspension Bridges 21

Fail Another Spit Test 22

Good Lighting is Important 23

Incident Report: Identifying Characteristics 24

Dream Specimen 62 25

Brock Street 28

Self-Portrait as a Leaky Boat 29

Seventh Floor 30

Incident Report: Location 31

Cranked Up 32

Dream Specimen 95 33

Market Research 36

Orphan of Overboard 37

Incident Report: Vehicle 38

Art Therapy 39

Self-Portrait as Sawdust 40

A Window That Won't Close 42

Air and Dirt 43

Every Day 44

On Not Knowing How She Got Home 45
or How Many Weeks She'd Been Gone

Autumn Takes its Rifle for a Walk 46

Dream Specimen 178   47

I Always Hear Songs Playing   50

Incident Report: Suspect Status   52

Stretch Your Arms Overhead   53
   and Your Body Will Know There is No Threat

Beautiful Children with Pet Foxes   54

We Are Small and So We Think Small   69

A Cauterizing Dawn   71

Incident Report: Assets and Belongings   72

Prorogation   73

The Mortgage Broker Asks for My   74
   Net Income from the Previous Year

Roofers   76

Dream Specimen 227   77

Incident Report: Injury Code   80

Self-Portrait as a Moth Reincarnated   81
   as an Oak Tree

Tasseography   82

Homalambulophobia—Fear of Touching   83
   or Walking on Flat Surfaces

Incident Report: Describe the Dwelling

Was the door locked?
Was the snow shovelled?
Were the leaves raked?
Was the grass cut?
Was the fridge full?
Was the food rotten?
Floor dirty?
Were there fire hazards?
Was the smoke detector keening?
Were there any pets?
Any furniture?
Was it overturned?
Was the sink clogged?
Traces of bodily fluids?
Did the toilet flush?
Was the laundry done?
Was the TV on?
Was the TV on mute?
Was the garbage out?
Were there weeds in the garden?
A car in the driveway?
Gas in the car?
Was there any mail?
Who was it for?
Were cockroaches on the counters?
Were there fleas mice bats?
Was there ash mould glass?
Were there any people in the dwelling?
Were there any other people?
Were there any other people?

Dinner Table

The one in the dining room, the one
my second husband made and under that,
a much smaller table. Under that,
seven frogs blinking their third eyelids
open and closed, open and closed.

The dead still sit and fold their hands
across from us. They try to tell us so much
we don't even listen anymore.
Too many plates need gathering up,
and these days, everyone's a soldier.
We just slide back the chairs
and pull the pillowcases
back over our heads.

I sweep my forearm across the silver clutter
and dash it to the floor.
This is my ceremony, backed by
seven tadpoles, seven caterpillars,
seven young girls in black
reclining in the doorway.

This is nation-building. I keep
a pet grouse on the verandah.
Together we tend the cocoons
and pour water over those who need it.
We peer into the night field
and see shapes move,
then don't see them.

Self-Portrait as a Mollusk

A red shell grows over my forehead,
across one eye, as my cheeks cave
in retreat, shielding the dark wet folds.
I'm bereft of speech and bone
and the ability to perceive distance.

Bi-valved, hinge-less,
I'm trying to rest in this spiral shell,
but last year has snuck in with me:
all those silver hallways
teeming with mothers.

Branches scrape my slime,
their dry hands reaching out
looking for lost daughters,
ones they gave away
or ones they should have.

The Stains I Scrubbed from the Floor

Cherries in my grandma's yard,
the trim around her windows,
the cistern cap. Safehouse.

The less common trillium:
trillium erectum, Wake-robin, Stinking Benjamin,
birth root, abortionist.

My preference in lipstick.
Rock lichen. Girls' knees.

The binding of my first Bible,
though I wanted black like the men.

The peeling skin on the barn.
What if nothing at all existed?

Nothing is its own colour, exiled.

The first time I smelled my own blood.
Every time since.

Very few gemstones.
A heavy steak before cooking.

The parrot's tail feathers and how I know
he will mock my voice after I die.

The faux-Moroccan lamp's glass panels.
Antarctica's primordial glaciers.

The stains I scrubbed from the floor
after the cops stormed the house again.

All my guilt, wineglass after wineglass.

The moon I remember looming
over the apprehensive lake.

Dream Specimen 23

I was lost
in a seething crowd
of breeding women
who sneered at me.

My mother, milk-eyed,
the only one to help deliver it
like a parcel on a porch.
More like a planet,
she said, made of lead and slop
that you have to push out
and send back into orbit.

A doctor showed me
a video of the baby
decaying and grey.

Transitional phase.
Fear of responsibility.
Deteriorating hopes.
Warning.

Rejection of creativity.
Indifference.
Self-deception.

Gaining significant amounts of weight
and choosing inappropriate clothing.

Bad timing.
Bad luck.

Feast of rest,
crunch hormone,
transplant fellatio.

Lieutenant to self-starter,
semitone to lifespan,
renaissance of crinoline.

Badger tin.
Washcloth, wallaby, lullaby.

Cult hotspot: cuckold hospital.
Galaxy silk. Trauma phoney.

You, too, are blasphemy.
You are too bleak.
You bleat.
You bleeder.

I Know My Own Limits and They Are Rigid

The thick, maroon whistle of a train
etching the far side of a mountain.
The rapids I refuse to cross.

Like a safe clanking shut, it occurs to me
in this black recliner, my window-frame diorama:
woodstove, sunset, hilltop, lakeshore.
A six-pack rainy afternoon game of Scrabble.

All the Halloweens I dressed up as
the dentist office waiting room,
the time wasted sorting buttons into piles,
the faith I have neither found nor yet inspired.

I know my own limits and they are rigid.

A dancer-like whitetail, flaunting agility,
leaps through snow—legs, twigs, ice.
Stops to pluck a still-living
shoot from the foot of a maple.

It's just that someday
I won't be in this chair anymore.

Others, watching an owl—
squat, neckless, ancient—
alight on the edge of the deck

will say *That was her chair*, and
Let's just leave the blinds open.

Wipe Clean the Sky

A cool, white mist
unspools, fills our
chipped blue mugs as
it spills the ruined sky.

The sun, disgusted,
has long since blinded itself
to the needs of others.

Now we wear the mist as a scarf,
the lake a magician's cape
and wish our third eye
would stop twitching.

Boil some eucalyptus leaves,
and twirl a new dance:
we clack our bones together
and roll down the hill.

The mist wishes instead
it was fire—
joining hands, reaching up
bright to help the sun
heal its Gloucester eyes.

But it's not, it's just
water's thin ghost
hovering over the lake.

When I Was Four I Put a Tent Pole Through My Cheek

Temagami, tearing down
camp and even then
an impulse to help the uncles.
To be taller. To be a red pine.
Silver tent pole aloft, teetering—
then my face rips open,
flames and
poisoned tentacles
and everything dirty
I ever thought
spurts out and everywhere
is a forest fire everywhere
is my face, burst,
sparks of my gleam
splattering like scales
overflowing my own edges,
the sky black glitter
I careen down the path
like a stampede
a terrible parade
the trees hacked down
and all the fish dead.

> The men grew lighthouse necks
> every face a searchlight
> slicing through me nights
> I'd rather drift alone
> on waves, my mouth wide
> to whatever I can catch,
> but all night long
> silver scales fell
> from my hot skin,

pine needles shook
from my hair
in soft chimes
as less and less
of me was left,
no wrist caught
in thick fingers
no arms to raise
against blows no legs
to crouch unseen,
just a blistering red moonface
with a big white hole,
marked.

Self-Portrait on a Tuesday

A little girl in a blue dress
vomits in the corner.
She might be me.
She tugs at her hair
with a tilt then quick
jerk of her head.
Excuse me, are you me?
She hands me
a fistful of her hair.
Looks down at the puddle
on the floor then back at me.
That doesn't answer my question
I say. It's Tuesday, she says
and I broke the little window.
Now all the hands
are going to get inside.
Never mind, I say
and hand her back
the hair. You're not me.
I always left the windows open,
the hands already
on the stairs.

Hypochondria

Everything is fine and then one day
a bit of blood when there should be none.
Fresh gratuity for the mosquito.
Wet rubies for the pipefitter.
Tulips aghast in the garden.

Honeybees nestle in lobbyist,
in bookie. My money's
on pollination. Things spread.
Have a look in today's corral.

A sticky orange row of bobbing polyps.
Militant, fertilized, eyeless.
Maws pursed, waiting
for their turn at my bones.

Suspension Bridges

Speaking of deathbeds,
a lady's always got room.
Here's another fatherland
hitch-hiking on my hemlines,
vying for legroom
with the townies and the nebulas.

My brass-tipped fingers tear
this government-issued wedding dress.
I'm a vigilante in the inner circle
of pepper spray. I hallucinate hoofbeats,
sidestep the riot cop. Truss up
the light stealing through branches.

Banal blasphemy, another codger
burning down the lighthouse.
Water's old mumbling—
ineffectual at best. Only the bridges
bother to listen. Townships and damned
insipid births, gurgling like
a wasps' nest, rotted wet
and debacle-heavy.

Fail Another Spit Test

There's a long line at the pharmacy.
I'm behind a woman in white,
gold toenails, legs bruiseless.
A seahorse squirms as she
holds it up like a torch.
Its left eye scans the crowd
while its right glares straight at me.

We've stood here all day.
There's a shadow behind the counter
but no one answers our shouts.
A man behind me quakes and foams.
Further back, a teenager throws up again.
Up ahead, someone falls to the floor
and stays there, still.

The line sways to the left
then right, as though we're at sea.
My eyes cloud over as steam
bursts from holes in the floor,
swallowing the light in soft gulps.
I lick the salt from my lips
as my skin hardens into bony plates
and my left eye drifts over the room.

Good Lighting is Important

The way you tilt your head
so a shadow slips over your face
like a hood, at precisely
the moment you lie.

The way the light flickers
as you swallow
the little noisemakers
in the tiny plastic cup,
or stash them like seeds
for another long winter.

The way you angle the brass lamp
to best ricochet off the dozen staples
you stamped in your husband's
scalp, like diamonds. Look.

The way the beams refract
and scatter into red, yellow, blue
shards splattered across your face,
proud, as the nurse explains
his skin, like wet tissue.

Incident Report: Identifying Characteristics

A mother who is a towering sycamore,
arms outstretched to block the sun
whose skin is fragrant bark,
dry and rough against my cheek.

A mother who is a pit of mud,
cool and soft, curling around me
when I fall into her, naked
and hungry and without memory.

A mother who is the sky,
wide with thunder
and bigger than the world,
shoving me over from behind.

A mother who is a volcano,
whose burning venom
carves her initials into the sides of mountains.
Who I might run from, or dive into.

Dream Specimen 62

Bright paths sinew
through shoulder-deep snow
to a crystallizing pond.

Wet plywood shacks
list and slump, injured
on the slush-edged shore.

Then four unusually large
paper-white fish swim by
and a sudden elation

surges up my throat
and I can't even
swallow it back down.

True intentions.
Achieving goals.
An excess of tranquility.

Positive changes are afoot.
Hard work lies ahead.
Economic prosperity.

Indirectly affecting
someone's illness.
A guilty conscience.

Malicious gossip.
Suppressed anger.
Old books.

Surgeons guess around.
Characters sabbatical.
Charlatans liken.

Wallpaper's shred-deficit,
backbone downgrade
sabotages productivity.

Parachutist statistician
stateroom to frenzy
surrogates of wallow.

Showcase defeatist—
peacock excursions
bullfrog and backfire.

Brock Street

Three white-tailed deer
on the sidewalk:
hooves polished, giddy rural expats
bored of leaves, martini-eager,
greedy for dancing.

Back home, a forest opens its fist.
In its palm, a clearing.
A barb-faced eagle
flies his shadow overhead.
First a kite, then a shroud.
Plucks a rabbit
from a little girl's lap.

We three skitter home at dawn,
as a Taser-hipped cop
wedges his boot onto
a man's neck. We shout,
click our camera phones,
file sprawling reports.

In the morning
the street is clean
and we are hungry.
We look down at our feet
and see our hooves
are caked with mud.

Self Portrait as a Leaky Boat

I'm the stainless steel handle
slouching on the bailing bucket
I'm a yellow tow rope
coiled on the floor
I'm the reeking sulphur
in the waterproof flare
I'm the life vest's plastic clasp
that doesn't quite close
I'm the needle in the compass
red tip bitten off
I'm a little orange whistle
crawling into your mouth
I'm the sudden winds
sneaking up lee side
I'm the heavy cloud
shuttering the moon
I'm a search party of one
my chapped hands empty

Seventh Floor

I am the newest arrival, still trundling up and down the runway.
This medical waste bin is the epitome of discretion,
of motherhood, of sauerkraut in the root cellar.
It has adopted me.

Here I make new friends fast.
What we have in common is our shine and elasticity.
We bounce from the backs of orderlies, frog skin
stretched to protect our glass-boned toes.

My roommate smuggles in a cell phone.
I call my children and they say things like
lacerations, charges,
lawyer, surety.

I rub my eyes and drop the phone.
I hear *masturbation, harpies,*
yearling, whirligig.

Incident Report: Location

The porch juts out like a sneer.
The name of a girl's father—
redacted—still paces
the sidewalk out front.

The attic crammed full
of everything I try to avoid:
the phone calls made too late
the hospital rooms unentered

the secrets nudged free
now tumbling down the stairs.
In the woodstove, I build a fire,
though I know what hides in ash:

fingernail, intake form,
snail shell, and bright
red embers, dressed up
and ready to go.

Cranked Up

Every night, broadcast through the building:
Your uniforms are not camouflage.
Just go to bed. Try to sleep through the night.

The dark: sleep refusing to get back inside.
Meaning that has long since packed up its meagre lugs
and moved on to the next day without you.

I pull on my boots and head downtown.
The ATMs are fallow, I've gulped the last of the Ativan,
and bacteria race up and down the steps

of City Hall, cranked up on anything they can find.
The streetlights flicker off when a bus collides
with a dark blue van. Blood vessels bloom,

tiny wet despots, occupiers of language,
as my night terrors stroll by,
holding hands and window-shopping.

That's it. Give me a new trap door,
a clean blanket, another fetid
father figure to crawl back under.

Dream Specimen 95

I'm alone in trees as the day dissolves
to a bright royal blue, glowing thick
and settling on the world like a balm.

I feel free and smile and throw
my arms wide like when no one
has betrayed you in a really long time.

Then a white pickup truck full of four bellowing bros
hurtles into the clearing, splinters the trees
and crumples right next to me.

Posture still perfect, their pale heads
ringed with blood like the crowns
they thought they already wore.

Desire for sexual stimulation.
Failed transactions with foreign syndicates.
Problems coming to an end.
A demand for better treatment.

Beware of false prophets.
The Four Horsemen of the Apocalypse.
A military strategy. A risky person.
A lack of respect.

Problems with relatives.
Adding to someone's pain.
Harbouring deep anxieties.
Denial.

Girl of ignore. Deflection apostrophe.
Tails are question to a curse,
handbag a diatribe.

Questionnaire to curtain-raiser.
Cover under thick bolts of cloth:
opinions, adoptions, abortions, cellulite.

Broadcast fist thrombosis,
new tracheas, a threat faucet.
Bluff gnats at the door.

Tales are quill to customer, box cutters to management.
Marble suit punishment. Clench whore verbs
in an ideology cul-de-sac.

Market Research

Tape on the foam mask.
Skid off to the next focus group.

Do you have wingspan envy?
Sudden tinnitus from taking flight?

Was your uterus deleted
from an apocryphal spreadsheet?

Rate your likelihood of revenge
from one to—just kidding!

Is the air too alkaline
to breathe? How about now?

Slogans soar and scatter.
Make a list of how you feel.

Storm voice. Bicycle bell.
Muscle spasms.

Do you wish the earth
were still flat?

Butterflied, tenderized.
Every direction, languid.

Orphan of Overboard

Underwater, I follow
the directives of gills.
Keep swimming. Fins
of dialect, fins of kinship.

A fishbowl to drain
myself into.
Whimper and bile,
buoyancy's salt crust.

Osteopath's end table,
motorboat, monocle—
waterlogged, listing,
awestruck.

Incident Report: Vehicle

Low rumbling surges
like a father.
I go to sleep
or am convinced
I'm sleeping.

At the party,
the bed in disguise.
Shame, a box
with a false bottom.

Not everything
that looks like a raft
will float.

Art Therapy

They haul me, woolen,
from cliffside to cold room.

I doze in the studio.
Judgment or décor,

dull knives and only
one colour paint.

Fistfuls of straw. Sweep
the children, wash the garden.

Tenderized denizen,
ward detritus.

All these miscarried thoughts.

My turtle shell bubbles
the snorts of horses.

This buzz sinks false.
I can't drown.

Cradle to lexicon
last will to diversion,

a gap between slats
to paint in the light.

Self-Portrait as Sawdust

Cut down to size
I'm little heaps
of warmth
swept from the shed:
stain remover
carpet cleaner
thief of spills
floorslut.

Urine-drenched
bedding for animals
when they bend one knee
then another then another
then another and sigh
staring out at
one white star
caught in a dark window.

A sedative when mixed
with warm milk
and honey, soaking up
torrential thoughts:
trees crashing through roofs,
children vanishing
like birds.

A filter for mercury
copper lead leering
in the garden
the rain barrel, the well
I hoard glittering
toxins, skin cold
pores gleaming.

A spleen, bile heavy
greed-swollen
three times its normal size.
Grab a sweaty fistful,
whatever gives you a better
grip, white-knuckled
in the parking lot.

A Window That Won't Close

The sun hides from me, leaves wilt
and my waxy sheen puckers like old fruit.
I shiver with nothing to pull over me
but a big silver room,
and a window that won't close—
cold stars rushing in.

I try to bargain with the past.
An overripe pear, its too-sweet skin
pulses, tears open, leaking oils
from my secret adolescence.
A box of crayons, melted,
under the car's back windshield.
Rays of light crumpled, boneless.

A stranger leaves a note curled
in a small brown bottle at the foot of my bed:

> *Red dress, stolen cabbage, second marriage.*
> *What's a few dropped stitches*
> *in the synapses. Here's a whip-thin tail*
> *for warding off fatigue. Pull away*
> *this backless smock, dance like your skin*
> *is a borrowed ball gown and all the stars*
> *will fly past, sucked back tight*
> *into their sockets.*

Air and Dirt

All along the roads:
stiffened cattle, sharp dust,
ranchers with lungs like dried-up canteens.

Hydro lines crackle,
then quiet. The sky lowers and clunks,
broken grain elevator.

Envelopes amass in mailboxes,
clone until the lid gapes.
Some flop to the porch like salmon.

Shade flanks the factory.
A small vine uncurls,
stretches, and scales the fence.

Every Day

We think the slugs will stop
chewing their way through the kale.
They leave holes bigger than themselves,
like dead movie stars.

Wet, hacked-off chunks of muscle.
Waxed and glinting frownless faces.
We're all just trying to be whole.

On Not Knowing How She Got Home or How Many Weeks She'd Been Gone

A fridge full of mould
ghost food in a ghost kitchen
a ghost of herself
worried down to half her size
trying not to remember
before alone, the house spotless
picking lint from the carpet
by hand. Now she sits, smokes
stares hard at the shadows
that show up then leave
as the sun outside
darts around the yard
she begins to count
each speck of dust
as it falls, each tiny
invader, subtle at first
then bolder, crowding in
she loses count as it piles up
filling in her ghost feet
then her ghost knees
then higher, not asking
her name or even
looking at her.

Autumn Takes its Rifle for a Walk

The coliseum, agape—miles of silent,
stoic rock, a half-frozen bog.

The dead-end trails promise footprints
but swindle their followers at dawn.

A prop plane bobs along the remains
of last night and still can't find its way back.

The wind rasps a cheer, waves
a union flag, is quickly shushed.

Mobs of moose march in threes along the road,
draped in shawls woven from dead leaves.

The first and last carry orange hats,
sodden and dripping, between their heavy jaws.

Unanimous, they veer right,
vanish into the hydro pass.

Artificial angle, accident of bone.
Another brittle spectacle. Cloud rattle.

Dream Specimen 178

A cold dim room brimming
with antiques clustered
on a dirt-packed floor.

A piano bench stacked
upside down on another
identical piano bench.

I grab its legs with both hands
and set it down,
right side up to sit on

but it lurches up on its own,
flips over and slams
down hard on top of its twin.

No piano, just dust dazzling the air
where the sun sneaks in
and I don't want to be afraid.

I pull the stool down again,
press its four legs to the ground
but it clatters back up fast,

as though magnetized. Angry.
Then my father is standing
at the back of the room and says

Touch nothing else.

Procrastination.
Discord.
Chaos.

An inability to connect with others.
Too much time alone.
Trapped.

A desire to understand worldly conflicts.
Unfinished emotional business
related to childhood.

A problem.
A terrible mistake.
Unexpected help.

Passive.
Helpless.
Useless.

Fighting off a virus or bacteria.

On typescript's torso
a think tank free-for-all.
Out of placenta, the same plagiarism.

Flotilla filibuster,
our old future
grafting its legislators.

Arbitrary curfew or jail,
Aspirin of your lifestyle,
another cop apologist.

I lost my felicities
under the childminder.
She'd threesome the impossible.

Something within my libido
my adulteress hoof,
thong freeloader.

Emotional butchery
can sequin without semi-circle—
anticipated nurture is below the meat.

I Always Hear Songs Playing

The fish shed their silver scales,
set the oracles adrift
and they surface. I pluck them,

glue them to my chest,
an offering to you.
You flick record on your phone

and slam the door as I turn away.
That silence that chokehold
that current in the room.

I never needed to have
telepathy or fish hooks
in the bath until I did.

I always hear songs playing
but you smirk and convince me
it's just the usual shrill

bird-squawk spin, reborn,
repackaged and on repeat.
Choruses an hour long

wrapped around my wrists
my ankles my neck, trailing
off, wispy octaves diving

in and out of cockpits. Tomorrow
I'll skewer myself awake
with the sharp gusts of air that

carry the past right by me,
all the songs distorted and
dropping through pitch-perfect light

violent and banal as
cold future winters
too much telepathy

an ice-polished fish hook
when you tell me I'm lying
or grin and ignore me.

Incident Report: Suspect Status

I crawl along a river
eavesdropping:
a doe's hind leg
stomps once, twice.
Here, there is food.
There, a stranger.

The deer scatter,
their shadows are
acrobats tumbling
behind them.
Boats drift in,
white sails snapping
in time with cold wind.

I'm camouflaged
on the beach, draped
in a wig like the sick,
furtive behind my most
polite-looking death mask.

The pharmacy, not
from parties or from
pathology at all.
Part vaudeville, part
floatation device.
What do they mean by
water bottle, anyway?

Stretch Your Arms Overhead and
Your Body Will Know There is No Threat

Sharpen the tip, and pin the ribbon
on any pigeon that can fly straight.
Wet feathers where the eyes once flared.

Truth a raven. Lungs going like pistons.
Once revered, now caged
and flapping hard.

All your failures
have their high school reunion
on your front lawn.

Might as well roll up the sod
and choose: which doors to prop open
and which to lock.

A swamp is still a swamp
and dirt will slur at its shores.
Step into the pocked road,

shield your eyes and scrape the sky
against your cheek as if to say
See? I can change.

Beautiful Children with Pet Foxes

Everywhere I look there are beautiful children
with pet foxes. The schools have closed
and the beautiful children with pet foxes
have taken over. They run through the streets
with their leashes, their bells, their inoculation forms,
some of them stumble while others snatch food,
all of them orphaned, the foxes all wild
and they are not ghosts at all.

I apprentice myself to the beautiful children
with pet foxes. I apprentice myself
to their wet eyes
their fluttering stomachs
their bloody noses
their hard and tiny fists.

I follow them, my childhood
a faint shadow. I practise
smiling when they laugh
or crying when they do, I pinch
the insides of my wrists and wonder
if I'm doing it right. I apprentice myself
to their scabby arms, their scratched cheeks,
the stench of fox urine in their beds.

I apprentice myself to the foxes,
to parabolic ears that teach me to hear
the footsteps of mice darting underground,
the twitches of insects that think
they are hiding. Green curtains
rustling in the wind by the deck,
the buzz of a 3am text:
Someone's gotten into the house

I apprentice myself to their enclosures
the doubly reinforced chain-link fence
jutting three feet down in the dirt,
I apprentice myself to the sand pit,
I apprentice myself to the holes
the foxes fling open and dive into.
I apprentice myself to the pacing

in glaring hallways where you see
yourself in the floor, puffier, sedated,
you but not you and you jolt—

They said I was uncooperative, that I refused food
that I would throw my tray on the floor

I apprentice myself to their skittering fleas
piercing through warm flesh.
I apprentice myself to insatiable thirst.
Fleas' disregard for claws and poison.
I apprentice myself to resilience and gluttony.

Twenty lengthy hospitalizations
five when I managed to visit
six varieties of restraints twenty-four
male cops (and one female) seven strip searches
five shifting nine-tailed diagnoses
one hundred and nine thousand tablets swallowed
three hundred and seven hidden in socks
in pillows, in potted plants—

I apprentice myself to the infestation.
Blood flicker static. Parasites.
Impassable hailstorm in every room.
I daughter myself to the doorway
as you tear off another layer of skin.

Someone is tampering with my pills

I apprentice myself to the dens they burrow into,
to the hum of soil and new names
for home. I apprentice myself to a dark
that smoothes sharp eyes and fur
on the backs of their necks, that tells them
which lights are on and which ones
are broken bits of sky
flashing in the yard.

I apprentice myself to the stillness,
to knowing where to sleep
and where to pounce.

Weird things keep happening here

Tonight a fire truck drove by
and the cardboard that was under
my water bottle is missing and I didn't

What do you think it means

I apprentice myself to hunger
to tracking earthworms in the yard after a storm.
I apprentice myself to arched backs,
a coiled strike, quick-snapping sinew

like locked doors hissing shut
opening only for meals, for pills, for television hours.

I apprentice myself to their jaws,
carrying around all those kits
without devouring them
or dropping them into the river
when the blurred days and weeks without dreams
stretch on like a mine shaft
and I apprentice myself to the letting go.

I can hear them in the attic now

They're tearing down the walls

Get them out of here

You've got to help me

Why won't you help me

Where are you

Where are you

Where are you

This is all your fault

Answer me

They're everywhere

Answer me

You never help me

You ruined my life

You're just like your father

You're just like your father

You're just like your father

I apprentice myself to the earthworms,
lungless, quaffing the air through their skin
as I drag around my ribcage full of dirt,
full of splinters, of stitches, staples,
caution tape, the old rocking chair,
the nurses, the lawyers, the judges,
the doctors who use the third person
even though you sit right there.

I apprentice myself to their brave eyeless tunnelling,
leaving a trail of nutrients that feed the dandelions
the beautiful children with pet foxes
pick for their mothers, hoping
that one day they'll come back home.
I apprentice myself to where the tunnel will pull me
how long to stay down there,
and how to keep my wet skin from stiffening
and locking me in its cold hull.

I apprentice myself to the way they sense light,
the menace of a warm touch to damp skin.

I'll learn to feel the glare
from your sunspots and know
when to slip into the shadow cast
when you pile the chairs
the tables the lamps the plants
into the centre of the room
and install another lock on the door.

I have to figure out how they're all getting in

I apprentice myself to the dandelions
the beautiful children with pet foxes
clutch by the fistful and hold up high
above the foxes' teeth.

I apprentice myself to sticky milk
in hollow popping stems, how it glues
the beautiful children's hands together
as though pleading, as though cold.
How it's harvested and pulped into rubber
and used to form the tires
that take you back, under flashing lights
to white rooms with no mirrors
or with way too many.

I apprentice myself to the tires,
to layers of carcass ply and steel belts,
deep tread for holding on,
bevelled edge for sharp corners,
unexpected twists of logic,
to stop you from sliding across black ice
on the highway then down the bank
plunging deep into night water.

I apprentice myself to thin green necklaces
made from dandelion stems
looped and chained together,
dripping down the necks
of the beautiful children with pet foxes.
I'll throw one into the water
and pull you to the surface,
I'll haul you up to the road
that I pave with the stones you fast disown:
arrest warrant, restraining order, bail hearing,
court support, legal aid, diversion, discharge.

I'm being framed

I could hear them in the waiting room

They said arson they looked right at me

They think I burned down that house

What should I do

Where are you

Why won't you call me back

I apprentice myself to their spread,
blazing yellow spits of sun:
milk witch, wet-a-bed, butter flower, dog-pisses
racing along the edges of the ditch.

I apprentice myself to the rites
the beautiful children with pet foxes
perform on mornings when the wind is still.
They rub sand on their faces
scrub their hands in the creek
tug mats from fur and untangle knots
woven through each other's hair.

Foxes quiet, ears cocked,
whiskers scanning the air for news,
the beautiful children with pet foxes
line up in a row along the bank,
braced for their mothers
to march over the ridge.

I apprentice myself to the sand
and all of its fervent ambitions:
how to smooth away splinters
how to stop a flood from creeping closer
how to melt into something sharp and clear and hard
how to hold the walls together
how to be a castle full of rooms
how to be the desert.

I apprentice myself to the stones
the beautiful children with pet foxes
pluck from the dirt and polish in their mouths
until they shine like the rings
their mothers slid off and left behind.
Some swallow the stones
to sit in their stomachs like anchors
so the beautiful children with pet foxes
don't float away into the sun.

Others stack the stones
into cold, narrow monuments
and I apprentice myself to their testimony:
each stone's knowledge of how to disappear
into something larger. How to be forgotten
by the mountains they're scraped from.
How not to shatter upon impact
when waking in an unfamiliar room,
the dirges masquerading as jubilees,
the mountains looking on mutely.

I apprentice myself to vigilance,
I stand up straight for days
until I crumble at the elbows,
shrug the sky loose and it tilts,
spilling frenzied crows into your yard.

The beautiful children with pet foxes
drink from the river every day
until the current mistakes them
for itself, tucking them into its folds
and rushing them downstream
as though they are late
for a very important ceremony.

There are birds in the kitchen flapping everywhere
I keep losing count of how many
I don't know how to get them out

I apprentice myself to the counting.
The number of tremors in a hand
the number of ghosts in a hallway
the number of daughters I should be.

How many daughters on the run
how many daughters locking doors
how many daughters in the curtains
how many daughters like it rough
how many daughters look away
how many daughters signing forms
how many daughters in the river
how many daughters in the mirror
how many daughters looking in—

I apprentice myself to the gaze,
take a few extra steps
away from the window and
save them for an emergency.

The beautiful children with pet foxes
are not sleeping well.
Too many shadows bob on the ceiling,
each one urgent and obscene
hissing loose a litany of secrets,
the foxes always keening,
the air too crowded for sleep
to find its way back in.

The beautiful children
stop feeding the foxes.
They won't clean the pens.
They don't let them out to run.
The foxes grown thin and matted.
They nip at each others' ears.
They pace. They pus.
Soon, there are fewer of them.

Then the beautiful children
throw open the gates,
pull out their pocketknives
and cut the foxes' collars.
They look away as the troop
runs across the dirt, one rippling mass,
and dissolves into the trees.

I'm thinking of selling the house

I can't stay here anymore

I apprentice myself to the pocketknives.
How to cut clean without tearing.
How to file jagged edges.
How to tighten the screws
that bind hinge to door.
How to wrench cork from bottle.
How to fold myself away.

After the foxes have gone
the beautiful children
walk up and down the river
trying to remember
what to do with their hands.

They wade into the water
and swim without anchors
and there are so many of them
they outnumber the sand
they outnumber the waves
they outnumber the rocks
and they are not ghosts at all.

We Are Small and So We Think Small

A puncture in my neighbour's tire,
one ice pick at a time. A blister
on each of my enemies' heels.
A leaky roof and an audit
for my absentee father.

All day long, I scour new policies,
sign the right forms, and wait cold
in the proper hallway.
Everyone else billows
impossibly clean sails.

For once, I should try something different:
light a candle, wear a dress,
crack open the windows. Stop staring
down the road. Counterfeit
shadows. The bears won't come.

A fistful of press releases
to patch all the holes.
Enough with the suicide notes,
the pre-nups, the warranties.
Bring me the glockenspiels
and peppercorns.

I'll throw the curtain wide,
zip up this prom dress,
blow out this match.

A friend of a friend is having an affair
with the next door neighbour.
He has a pool. She says
she's bored. She is often ill
and no one knows why.

A Cauterizing Dawn

There's a hill outside and I lie on it,
this moss a jacket, the damp like knowing
the shiver of someone else's death.

A bear shuffles by,
yellow bird perched on her thick haunch
and I extend my palm to catch
the feathers tossed as they pass.

I turn and rub my nose in the dirt,
inhale the grizzly's last dream,
though all I can smell is my own sweat,
torn stitches, and another sleepless night.

What I think the bear remembers:
a pinch of rot in her nostrils
then a wet furless creature, mud for skin,
trying to snatch the birds right out of the air.

Incident Report: Assets and Belongings

Woodstove: caging fire
in a squat black box
like a once-feral pet.

Fire: expert appraiser
doesn't know its own age.
Advocates infinity. Heresy.
Rely on it but don't trust it.

Heresy: throw open the door to the river,
maroon all thoughts of tumours.
More and more televisions will arrive,
hauling their suitcases up the porch steps.

Suitcases: phones and clocks,
chargers and remote controls
revising their wills,
denying all permits,
erasing names from the land registry.

Doze on the couch,
lungs thickening.
Breath: shoaled—
distended reef-dweller.

The tiniest of movements—
eyelash flicker, protein
mutation—unnoticed.

Prorogation

Hedge fund fraud, lopsided lungfuls
of chlorine, age-appropriate forgeries.
Nothing worth mentioning happens in the past.

Can't blame the gill-necked clergy
for swimming away.
The government governing in absentia.

A mail-order snowstorm, returned to sender.
Clouds chug along the skyline,
pushing at the flanks
of the slow among them.

The rest of us must learn
to swallow hard, grow extra ribs,
and go all exoskeleton,
just to cross the finish line
intact.

The Mortgage Broker Asks for My Net Income from the Previous Year

One frantic downpour phone call
several million drops of rain
three stricken siblings
four hours fishtailing
two different hospitals
thirty-six stitches
thirteen staples (for luck!)
one missing hatchet
and we three deserters
dreaming of our own cold bunkers
deep down under the dirt.

One small-town police station
glinting quartz-like
among a thousand marching rows
of corn, tobacco, canola
one smirking front desk cop
two plexiglass eyes flickering
cold wet gun rot
my name in his mouth and
Do you want me to bring her up?

Desperate, I show off
my two double-jointed thumbs
then slide six lit torches
down my throat
like a citizen, like a taxpayer—
Is this what you mean
by resale value?

Two looming leanmeat morning cops
one hour early as I shower
off the previous day
hoping I'll dry into
someone else, someone kind
with actual feelings
maybe a vegetarian
or a washcloth
I yell to my brother
Go get my clothes!

The cops' laughter
like high school, like six more
kicks to the gut amid
fifty feet of yellow tape
two tall shadows leering close
and *Please, sit down*
No thanks, I say
I'll stand and I stand
and stand and stand
and stand and stand
and stand and stand
and I'm still standing.

Roofers

Tearing off old shingles, flinging them down.
Giant moths scuttling the sky.

The wings turn mid-air
into scarves and float gently.

No—they inflate like parachutes, dropping
more and more soldiers onto the sidewalk.

Troops barrel like trains through streets
rustle the nylon into mile-long cozies for pipelines.

Soon the whole country is wrapped in orange,
even the drones and the missing ballot boxes.

My dog shimmies close.
He dislikes tarps and kites

and other matters of flutter.
He nudges me toward the house

as if to say, Yes, we all want
to be better, to rip away a layer,

throw it in a dumpster and
smooth a new dress over the mould.

But we're running out of fabric,
and coastlines and things we can burn.

Here's another clean new nail,
another bucket of tar.

Dream Specimen 227

A tiny pair of gold earrings—
horseshoes in a plastic baggie
like you'd buy drugs in.
From jewelry store to jewelry store
I searched for a specialized technician
to convert them from gold into silver.

I had a partner. We were quiet and serious.
The earrings were not just earrings
but part of a covert operation
and they were urgency. I pretended
to really like them.
There was a war going on and
ours was a very important mission.

Happier times.
A hidden talent.
Unusual success in all enterprises.
An invitation to a high school reunion.
A waste of energy.
A stressful home.

Pay attention to your Adam's apple.
Be wary of external shine.
Don't stop to meditate.
Mind your own business.
Keep embarrassing memories to yourself.
Your boundaries are changing,
whether you like it or not.

Trespass guffaw. Topographic treasure map.
An over-accessorized
haystack, hazard, handicraft.
Vitamin gorge.
Pariah headband.
Ear slander.

Mentors, bone-in,
audition for groin marketing.
Opticians and opossums in homeopathic voice-overs.
The coward operetta.
The banjo strings tethering them together.
The semiotic analysis of my latest
unsolicited dick pic.

Incident Report: Injury Code

Without provocation, the leaves rise up
and fly to the wind's border.
Whisper something.
Then three trees tear up from the dirt
cracking like ribs.
Roots pried apart.
Naked, splayed.

A wet stench spreads.
One trunk leans, saplings bent
under its drunkweight,
suspended, double-dared
over the perfect house next door.

Mother runs horrified marathons
down horrified hallways
through horrified forests.
Asks me to tear off
bits of flesh from her
ankles and I do it.

Knotted fists, knotted branches,
knotted manes. A welcome home
banner snapping in the wind.

Splintered mother, folded
mother, lonely mother:
the fence is broken, horses out
and charging down the road.

Self-Portrait as a Moth Reincarnated
as an Oak Tree

Once, I could float down a staircase.
A procession of blue beads,

my wings' finest comet tail.
Now I'm tangled in the dirt,

stuck. Wipe clean the sky like a mirror
and watch my leaves leap

free, as though they have
somewhere at all to go.

Tasseography

My grandmother smashes my wineglass
and reads the shards like tea leaves.
She says life is full of flies
and questions and under the dirt,
more dirt. The larvae she plucks
from my mouth harden in the light,
knock against each other like marbles.
She hands me a sack full of rocks
all named after dead strangers,
each painted a different colour:
Famine. Factory. Father. Firing squad.
The glass fragments line up,
sweep themselves into a pile
and reassemble back in her fist.

Homalambulophobia—
Fear of Touching or Walking on Flat Surfaces

Define fear.
Define touching.
What about touching with an object.
Define walking.
Define escape.
Define pictures of mountains.
Define papering your room
with pages torn from library books.
Define your bed.
Define rocks and shoals of pillows.
Define flat.
Define gouges in the ceiling
from the garden hoe.
Define the prairies.
Define pregnant
and asking for money.
What about asking with an object.
Define in-utero.
Define in-utero trauma.
What were you wearing.
Define Tell them you made it up.
Define smile
leaning out the window
then sucked back in like air.

Notes and Acknowledgements:

Several of the poems in this book have appeared in various publications, often in earlier forms: *The Rusty Toque, Taddle Creek, The Humber Literary Review, This Magazine, HOOD, Cosmonauts Avenue, Riddle Fence, Arc Poetry Magazine, The Week Shall Inherit the Verse, Ryga: a journal of provocations* and *The Puritan*. Thank you to those editors for their attention and care.

Some of these poems began with or emerged from lines written after, between, or in response to work by Kim Hyesoon, Adrienne Rich, Anne Sexton, Sina Queyras, Rae Armantrout, Frank O'Hara, Selima Hill, Eduardo C. Corral, Brenda Shaughnessy, Mary Ruefle, Lisa Robertson, Nicanor Parra, Jen Currin, Gwendolyn MacEwen, and Matthew Zapruder. Work by many other poets inspired and sustained me during the process of writing this book.

"Brock Street" was part of a series of poems about Parkdale, commissioned for inclusion in the Synthesis gala fundraiser in support of the Queen West Art Crawl in 2011. The event put artists working in different disciplines together to respond to one another's work. I was paired with artist Andil Gosine, whose installation "Rum and Roti" was created in response to my series of poems about the Parkdale neighbourhood, where I lived for a tremendous decade.

Much gratitude to the following for their encouragement and counsel as early readers: Erik Culp, Kate Sutherland, Kevin Connolly, and Julia Tausch.

Thanks to Jay MillAr and the participants in his Long Poem Workshop, where the poem "Beautiful Children with Pet Foxes" began and was fostered with care and integrity.

High fives to Dani Couture for responding to my eleventh-hour SOS with editorial acumen.

A big outpouring of gratitude to Brecken Hancock for her astute and insightful editorial work on these poems. Her close, careful, smart and sensitive reading and excavations made these poems so much stronger. It was a pleasure to work together, and a pleasure to be encouraged to push still weirder and darker.

For their enthusiasm, commitment and dedication to poetry and community and risk and beauty, I thank Jay and Hazel and everyone involved with BookThug. Long after swapping our mid-1990s handmade litzines (*dig.* and *HIJ*), publishing this book with BookThug feels like a homecoming.

Thank you to the Ontario Arts Council's Writers' Reserve program and the Canada Council for the Arts for financial support that enabled me to focus on writing and rewriting this book.

SHARON HARRIS

JENNIFER LOVEGROVE is the author of the Giller Prize–longlisted novel *Watch How We Walk*, as well as two poetry collections: *I Should Never Have Fired the Sentinel* and *The Dagger Between Her Teeth*. In 2010, LoveGrove was nominated for the K.M. Hunter Artist Award for Literature and in 2015, her poetry was shortlisted for the Lit POP Awards. Her writing has appeared in numerous publications across North America. She divides her time between downtown Toronto and rural Ontario.

Manufactured as the First Edition of
Beautiful Children With Pet Foxes in the Spring of 2017
by BookThug.

Distributed in Canada by the Literary Press Group:
www.lpg.ca

Distributed in the US by Small Press Distribution:
www.spdbooks.org

Shop online at www.bookthug.ca

BOOK
PRODUCTION
WAR ECONOMY
STANDARD

Edited for the press by Brecken Hancock
Type + design by Kate Hargreaves
Copy edited by Ruth Zuchter